Vociferate

詠

Emily Sun was born in Hong Kong, moved to England at age three, and at eight years old immigrated with her family to Whadjuk Noongar Boodjar (Perth, Western Australia). Emily's poetry and prose have been published in various journals and anthologies including *Meanjin, Growing up Asian in Australia, Cordite Poetry Review* and *Australian Poetry Journal. Vociferate| 詠* is her debut poetry collection.

Vociferate

詠

Emily Sun

FREMANTLE PRESS

For my mother
&
my two grandmothers:
Wong Tai Mui (黃大妹)
Lucy Chang Ro Lan (张若兰)

'I have begun with the assumption that the Orient is not an inert fact of nature'
—Edward Said, *Orientalism*.

CONTENTS

BEGINNING ...

ORIGINS

let's see how we want our story to unfold
从前有一个小妹妹.

it should be a trip ... ...
                    ... ... to piece together
flows of stories
... drifting ... pondering
                    discovery
... ... social introspection ... travel ... love

agape as well of course
        and heartache
the heart must bruise until
after the inevitable climax.

                    topics and chapters need some working out
                    themes. how should we collate it.
                    one larger project.

we need to discuss this properly.
                    fiction? memoir?

Perspective?

                                        it's theirs not ours
            we have yet to experience insurmountable loss

                Il faut que jeunesse se passe

                there has always been loss.

从前有一个小妹妹 chung chin yau yat go siu mui mui (Cantonese) – once
    upon a time there was a little girl

CAUSEWAY BAY

Before there was
a 2047
baptised collectives
did not settle

Kashmir
Palestine
Hong Kong.

Home is a memory reinforced
        spun from the ethereal

大丸
placebo playground
grows an economy
even with the sun setting on the union jack

Pretty in pink and tartan skirts
and baby FM boots
distractions grow economies
built on land, speculative elation

There is no rhyme
only reasons why
we fly and float
to your shores.

大丸 daai yun (Cantonese) – big pill[1]

MAYBE IT'S WANCHAI?[2]
For 伍姑娘 & 云姐姨婆

Tape deck, SONY
made in Japan
too many places and too many dark spaces
soft wave radio
white noise comforts in mah-jeh's refuge
masking the sounds of a forgotten city

Non-recyclable plastic and metal, magnetic tape
Tony Leung pre-lust but with caution
together we unspool the tangles and with an
octagonal pencil, made in the people's republic,
rewind
re-spool
until the music plays
the 香蕉船 song
tonic to sub-dominant fragment
then the world started laughing
when I tried to start a joke there were
too many men in skinny flared jeans.

香蕉船 heung jiu syun (Cantonese) – banana boat[3]

ROMEO WOULD, WERE HE NOT ROMEO CALL'D

gifted with the radical
a foundation
of written culture
traded for Wuthering Heights
because it was too difficult for
everyone else
a good industrious Christian name
but more Germanic than Jesus.

no Germans were in the mountain
when Wei developed her principles eight:

点 dian, a strange stone
横 heng, a jade table
竖 shu, an iron pillar
钩 gou, crab pincer
提 ti, horsewhip
弯 wan, the horn of a rhinoceros
撇 pie, bird pecking
捺 na, press and wave[4]

but *my* eternal, *my* forever looks like
the carcass of a dragon fly.
people demand a refund for my
jade table and whip
for I dare not dig my spurs into the horse.

AH! VOUS DIRAI-JE, MAMAN[5]

don't go.
… he takes the eldest to a safer land
mother's sensually
smokey eyes now smudged by sadness.

    … shoeless girl
poor little rich girl
everyone else's

    memories of her Saigon father
将美金
挤喺
埋喺
藏喺
腊肠里面

now works in a hospital
not a nurse, nor a doctor.
in America they call them janitors.

the domestic returns home
unshaven breakdown of
protein, sweaty smells of unwashed
clothes of cinnamon,
bromhidrosis, osmidrosis, ozochrotia

no longer perfumed
nor in tailored dresses
with imported fabrics from Paris

将美金 jeung mei gum (Cantonese) – American dollars

挤喺 jai hei (Cantoneses) – squeeze

埋喺 maai hei (Cantonese) – bury

藏喺 chong hei (Cantonese) – hide

腊肠里面 laap cheung leui min (Cantonese) – inside Chinese sausages

never raged
that she'd leave school
(no one wants an overeducated wife)

now she empties an accountant's garbage
for a living.

LONG GROVE

一九八四年
back and forth
back and forth
back and forth
白痴

silly simpleton
halfwit dunce
clod
cardigan wrapped
by nurses
Edwardian asylum
黐线院.

far from the great hall
sequestered royals (血太近 呵!)
Polish people
war traumatised (conveniently)
forgotten footmen

the woman sees
the visitor and waves

we rock
back and forth
back and forth
back and forth
perpetual motion

I giggle.
She laughs.
Remember the apple trees of 狼高苦?

一九八四年 baat sei nin (Cantonese) – 1984
白痴 baak chi (Cantonese) – simpleton
黐线院 chi sin yun (Cantonese) – mental asylum
血太近呵 hyut tai gan la (Cantonese) – 'blood too close ah'
狼高苦 long go fu (Cantonese) – transliteration of 'Long Grove'[6]

BEDTIME STORIES

For Sun Chi Ying

the beginning of a new empire
on a small stretch of forest clearing
two freshly decapitated heads on a stake
calm, clean-shaven, eyes half-closed
sad faces in the middle of a narrow mud road
children walking past
the sentry unimpressed.
two thirds of a rainbow

faint in the post-monsoon sky.
hope hid in the blue eye of the South China Sea.

Momotaro-san, Momotaro-san
Okoshi ni tsuketa kibi dango!

they were great cyclists and
kind to the children they orphaned.

he never saw them
bayonet the children
the villagers did that
after Nagasaki.

… the daughter of a collaborator
        was left to bleed out next to her mother
        until someone said she was only adopted

Banbanzai, banbanzai,
O-tomo no inu ya saru kiji wa,
Isande kumruma on enyaraya![7]

REDHILL, REIGATE

clichéd bowl haircut
mini mongolian mozart me
gold medallion in hand
sodden music scores

no walker.
no refuge from rain
no bus
a green wagon circles
once, twice
no choice but to
accept a lift.

a pub
the native's world
warm. light
dries fears. laughter

RH1 or RH2?
It doesn't matter
white knight
yeast, barley
malt and hopes
brew in the air.
Friendly faced natives

disillusionment will come later:
it begins with coal and
national fronts follow.

HIGH TEA

Beat an egg
Mash a banana
Add flour
Oil
Beat again
Add sweeteners to taste
In Guyana add a spoon of sugar
In Malaya try condensed milk
In Australia stir in Vegemite
In New Zealand, manuka honey
[mash kumara instead of banana]
Bake until it looks edible
Plate it and
Drink it with Lady Grey.

Lord Grey is too busy with his cabinet,
And Napier, the sheep-farming
Bagpipe-mending flautist and navigator
Who intends to conquer superintend a
Celestial Empire.

LORD EWART'S STREET

arrival in the valley of filled-in
tarred streets off
great eastern
highway homes on quarter-acre blocks
later a VHS store
chaplino moustache
a gun mart alongside
broken homes

we slept with the doors unlocked
our neighbour hated japanese
thus we were safe

walked to school barefoot in summer.
past a broken home with broken people.
smiling faces until the time
a teacher voyaged to the moon.

a boy was dragged across the desk
by sir
a girl broke
another sir's arm
he carried it in a sling.

I copied words and more words from
the chalkboard. running
writing something about captains and banks.
drew pictures of botany I'd never seen
sang school songs about condemned convicts
a self-fulfilling prophecy.

was it even supposed to be ewart or did
someone deaf confuse them with tuarts?

there was one red gum tree
an asbestos house
in the wetlands now wasted.

BACKYARD SMELTERS

Without this rock I would starve
    Not be here
    Not *here* here

I would be elsewhere away from circles
    Merry-go-rounds on sea or land

This rock makes bridges and bullet trains
    dresses parvenus in emperor's clothes

It's true we cannot eat rocks
    but we can eat green bananas turned black
    digest money
    then see it as digits on our screens and
    these digits mean everything.

JUNE IS NOT WINTER

It is only so because the English said so when
they turned the globe upside down
and filled the lakes with imported meadows.

lok yuet, Juin, liu yue.
sixth month named for Juno,
goddess of marriage
architect of a modern institution that outlaws incest
yet mother of inbreds: Mars, Minerva and Vulcan.

Mother Goddess

Not so long ago, those who called this time of year
Magguro happily went about their lives without
ancient Gothic pulp fiction
soap operas with cast in togas.

They knew it was warmer inland.

TOXIC CHILDHOODS

in the end
the plush toys will be thrown out
new plastics recycled
into even newer plastics but not her.
she is more a danger to us than we first thought
It isn't her lack of genitalia
her peroxide hair
blue eyes
porn-star breasts
skin whitened

made somewhere in Asia
Hong Kong or South Korea?

she is too full of polypropylene
PVA, EVA and bendy plastics
safer than the lead and cadmium tin
soldiers from
the nutcracker suite.

What would the western swamp turtle say?

1989

the foetus is Taylor Swift
no one remembers the day *the* Ayatollah died

Can't stop
        Empower
                Shake
                Hate
                Fake
                Shake
                Shake
                Shake
the
System
                of the

                        down

                                a homeless motherland

        concrete parks and towers poured
                                easily onto, over, and in lawn. grown
        in many lands

                        embalmed corpses suffocate
        turn to wax
                        in glass coffins

        Voyeurs still line up in the smog

        Peep over the bamboo curtain after
                the iron falls

        A web is born.

怪怪了

strange child
怪怪了

    when you wander and wonder
    on your path as the
ugly child
乖乖了

    when you look in the mirror and
    see that
    you are too
jaundiced a child
怪怪了

    afflicted and diseased
    much like a
dead child
乖乖了

for pale grey
    hopes and blossoms in
    late autumn

别担心

怪怪了　guài guài le (Mandarin) – weird[8]
乖乖了　guāi guāi le (Mandarin) – obedient
别担心　bié dān xīn (Mandarin) – do not worry

NOBLESSE OBLIGE

Asia was tied down, face down
but she could still move the tips of
her toes. loosen bindings.
wriggle room for one century or was it more.
too much of her to swallow
whole.

a city (my home) born of violence.
like the mother weeping for the day
her son forces a girl's thighs gently
with his knees
and moans as he eases into her.
she's not ready but adapts
it's good when he increases his pace
slams into her. if she allows
this stranger access to her body, a follow-up
date will ease her fear of contracting an STD.
and one day, one day, she may want him.
syndrome of Stockholm y'know.

closing her eyes as he turns her over
and forces her to look when he moves
into her again.
at least he is clean. decent infrastructure
monarch-endorsed laws
he pecks her on the cheek and promises
she's better off with him
than the Portuguese.

                    120 or so years later, their descendants
                       will debate whether or not it was love.
                 and if it wasn't, what does it matter now?
                                    'there was added value'.

for others subject to
home invasions,

                there was no mercy

                    violence.

                            tearing. membranes.

                                memories.

                                      meaning.

OVER THE MOUNTAINS AND FAR AWAY

Only women are *sik bun* my grandmother says
she's seen how men like
my almost lover treat
loose women
who wander beyond their boundaries
unbounded.

You are not the same as him, she reminds me
There are mountains between our villages
even though we now live on flatland
with paved roads where
at the elm street is the beginning of elm street.

Unions between us and them are doomed
Look what happened to your uncle.

How can I argue with that logic?

IMPROMPTU

too young for concertos
dark sounds that came from
the ids of Teuton minds
performed by Teuton hands.

阿里山的姑娘
a simple girl, along the stream
a girl before industry
in a place
高山青 涧水蓝.

阿里山的姑娘
could have drowned in the stream
and we only saw her singing
with her beloved.

inside she was Schumann's
a minor raging with passion
and confusion,
disorientation,
and without serotonin reuptake inhibitors
the timpani pounds her brain
no elation in the song of joy
of peace
of understanding.

she dances along because she must.

阿里山的姑娘 ah lǐ shān de gū niáng (Mandarin) – The Maiden from Alishan
    Mountains[9]
高山青涧水蓝 gāoshān qīng jiàn shuǐ lán (Mandarin) – alpine green, water blue

CULINARY INTERPRETATIONS

there is rage, passion,
misery, misogyny,
abuse, misery,
unbalanced diet
in gloomy landscape
heather
the moors

warm wine and gingerbread, heating spices, cake,
cold wine, sugar candy, more wine, crusts, remnants of breakfast,
goose bread
sits on the table for an hour, milk, water and gruel, tea, more
crust, sugar and milk
leads to poor gut health
too little serotonin production

Joseph ate well
toasted oat cake and a
quart of ale.
he survived the story.

Heathcliff *was* a lost Chinese princeling
good with money
took over two properties
he looked like an angry Keanu Reeves

if only Nelly were more experimental with her cooking
if only the English liked rice as much as they liked tea
complex carbohydrates regulate your moods.

tragedy could have been avoided had the promise
of apples been fulfilled.

BRIEF OVERVIEW

Nietzsche was a Wagner fan
God is dead
        The superman [not uberman]
His sister was a Nazi
Hitler was a fan.

Marx played the stock market
Capitalism is eternal
        shaved his beard
Engels paid for his tomb.

Freud was an addict
saw genitalia in everything
death drive; sex drive
        he never reached menopause.

Darwin is why the sushi shop owner
        does not believe in organ donation

it is the survival of the fittest
        which is why they will foreclose his shop.

        The origin of species was cruel.

VOCIFERATE

what she really wanted was to be paganini
       the mad bad lord byron or deaf ludwig van
    for no one ever said *he* had a resting bitch face.

what she really wanted was blonde hair and blue eyes
    high cheekbones and higher brows so that the
teen boy sitting in the back row would stop calling her pancake
face.

what she also really wanted was to stop
    the dilettante from explaining
       what she already knew.

what she really wanted was to not butter her bread
    to sandwich statements for those who wanted her
       to stay small and succulent.

what she really wanted was legislative change
    so she needed no excuse to give her baby *her* name.

what she really really wanted was to wield wùkōng's
    rúyì bang and neptune's trident.

三从四德!!!

it's just as well she got some of what she wanted
or she would have been known as a Dragon Lady,
Goddess of Castration …

                 Vagina Dentata.

三从四德 sān cóng xì dé (Mandarin) – three obediences, four virtues[10]

SIX TWO SIX[11]

Introitus

darkened house.
roller shutters down.
no dog barks.
no cat meows.
no baby cries.
no one home.
waves crashing.

few buddhists attain eternal rest
perpetual light is blinding.

Kyrie

跑 跑走
快啲呀
跑呀跑呀
走呀走呀
东南西北
中发白

sprint speed
shin splints
pedal to the metal all the way
to ED

red light
green light
red light

drive carefully
mobile phones off
mercy, have mercy
merci.
grief-gorged eyes
hers or yours?

through the gates
cross the pale pink partition
the threshold where they stick you
with needles like a slab of meat
that beautiful androgynous man with the transylvanian accent
he'll be the death of me.

跑 跑走 paau paau jau (Cantonese) – run run go
快啲呀 faai di lah (Cantonese) – hurry up
跑呀跑呀 paau ah paau ah (Cantonese) – run ah run ah
走呀走呀 jau jau (Cantonese) – go ah go ah
东南西北 doong naam sai bak (Cantonese) – cardinal points (East, South, West, North)
中发白 joong faat baak (Cantonese) – central wealth white[12]

Dies Irae

across town parking lot.
are you leaving?

                                 a woman steps out of the car.
                                        brown car passes.
                                     red car takes its spot.

didn't you see us waiting there?

                                               no.

this was our parking spot.
                big hair, chromatic ruby cardigans.
this was our bloody parking spot.

                                  don't you swear at me.
shit.

                                  don't you swear at me.
fuck.

                                  don't you swear at me.
the coarsest word in the english dictionary.

                    gentle vietnamese woman screams
                        thumps their windscreen
                            quantus tremor

                                      I'll call the police.
I'll call the police.

                          dies irae, dies illa
                    solvet saeclum in favilla.

Tuba mirum

patience patient
a man with a beetroot face.

                      I've been here for five hours …

…

                      no one likes an angry woman.

Go away.

                      my heart aches

Then stay.

                      Are you sick?

No.

                      Your mother?

No.

                      嬤嬤

…

                      Very sick?

…

                      I lost my whole world

…

                      I've been there.

creation and death are eternal
this is the calm for the broken hearted.

嬤嬤 mama (Hokkien) – paternal grandmother

Rex Tremendae

her eyes plead stay
restless are the voiceless
roll of eyes
weakened.
face flattened
control over facial muscles
analysis paralysis.

Recordare

fermented century
eggs and burnt jook
plastic bowls are cheap and burnt.
I am a hungry ghost.

the manager is surprised to see me with a mother
could a 香蕉 girl who eats at 2am
with a boy on his 550c
be a filial slut?
we source our skins from the
good women of China.

we sit in silence
there is only common blood
no common tongue

MSG tickles my memories
page-three girls
louvre catalogue
breasts, I warned my friends
hairs in strange places
this is our destiny
there's no turning back
tantus labor sit cassus.

香蕉 heung jiu (Cantonese) – banana

Confutatis

please enter the house of Addams.
Morticia on pot.

what do you mean no op no op no op?

palliative care

Uncle Fester is at work.

pale pink curtains
pale
pink
cold
pale pink cold legs
111 beats per minute
130 beats per minute
galloping horses
140 beats per minute
race horses
150
galloping
galloping
galloping.

Lacrimosa

chest infection
bed sores
laboured breathing
dying is a lonely affair.

jelly food
was she socially isolated?
she was the life of the party but
we hadn't spoken for months.

help her in her final condition.

she dies on a red sky morning
before it turns blood orange
this first dying is in D minor
but the Daoists turn it pentatonic.

she dies on a red sky morning
inside my head
cacophony of resounding silence.

music ceases
to explain.

... WANDERING ...

Quiet on set. Rolling. INT. A CHINESE RESTAURANT. Off screen: hysterical 事头婆 screams at the chef who stands at the window chopping BBQ pork, chicken and duck. 'No heart, no heart, you have no heart' she cries in a non-existent, pan-Asian immigrant accent, more glamorous when set south of Canal, steam ring from the street. He ignores her even when she screams that she is the love child of Marco Polo, and he must give up his job to stay with her. She will lose face when she is forced to move into her son-in-law's Bel Air mansion. Lanterns. There must be red lanterns and chopsticks, and beautiful waitresses in loose fitting silver cheong-sam, the manageress in black, side slits to her upper thigh. The chef must be played by one of the Tony Leungs. The kitchenhand can be anyone ... as long as they are Asian. Cut.

事头婆 si tau por (Cantonese) – boss lady

BAK KUT TEH ON WUYISHAN

remember how timidly you threw the word out
into the conversation
about laksa
'because you ___ me so much!'
and then the betrayal.
it happens at all ages but the first
stab sears and bruises
residual ache that only
laughs when our RAM is rewritten
in middle-age.

you said that your ancestral village
was too low lying and that
mine was too high, fecund mountains
that grew tea
that started opium wars
yours was coastal, populated by
fishermen and merchants
who fled wars for richer lands
and only married their own
this explains your habsburg jaw

my village is now a tobacco plantation
but it doesn't really matter now anyway.
the marlborough man is dead.

WATERLOO

a beautiful man
handsome in rags
undeniably exquisite facial structure
crunches crisps
on the Burger King balcony

he is as unattainable as Juliet
unapproachable
proposition

unless you are the willowy blonde
with impossible grace

he descends and at ground level
he encircles the girl
an eyebrow raised
pupils dilated
a flash of light
nostrils flared as he strokes his lapel
swaggers towards the platform
Vogue perfect
will meet thrift-shop chic

but guards stop his
mating ritual
he and his unattended bag
taken away.

I recount my encounter with the exotic
at Ealing Broadway
we find another karaoke pub
the other was blown up by the IRA

we sing Zombie anyway.

KINDA LIKE A COUNTRY & WESTERN SONG

she told him that I crashed my car
drove into another at the red lights
it was at an intersection of leeches.

she never passed on his message
because she suspects he's my lover
and unlike my GP
does not think me too innocent.

what do you call someone
you can say anything to
and it feels so right
but it can never be because
he's made plans with another girl
I'm the 坏女人

he's just a man
like Clinton, 阿婆 says
we are all Hillarys

it's difficult to imagine 阿公
a human with legs
that took him places
and neurons inside
the skull firing commands
or with a reproductive system
to propagate the species
… eventually me
when they only memorialised his
head on a plate.

I wanted to ask her about her sex-life
啊呀…可惜 grandmothers in my day were post-sexual

坏女人 pai za bo (Hokkien) – bad woman
阿婆 ah por (Cantonese) – ah grandma
阿公 ah gong (Cantonese) – ah grandpa
啊呀…可惜 aya … hor sik (Cantonese) – unfortunately

BILLY WAS JUST A KID

high on pot, Nirvana was already dead
knife fight
with Mexicans
illegals who sowed and
reaped for
old money
profits on onions and cows
ranch steak.

claimed they went up to him
sliced his upper eyebrow
through his eyebrow ring
outside
a saloon when the west was young
when there was no law

I am in a Sundance film
A Butch Cassidy with a pallid wife
in a country for old [white] men
uncast and in the audience
I wove myself into their narrative
an exotic love interest
best viewed on Eastman Kodak
film calming influence on
the impetuous protagonist who threatens
to kill my lover
Miss Saigon has to die but that was before
Ho Chi Minh

a God-fearing lover in God-fearing land
kicked by his congregation
an exorcism for all sinners
lost in Death Valley
Aliens emerge from Area 51
a nerved host high on his own nostrum

shows me a stockpile
of semi-automatics
and brags about a hit list.
The Mexicans, they say, are waiting.

I should've asked for an understudy
to play the girl who stares into
his sea-green eyes
this space is not for me.

I'll ask for the girl at the Panda Express.

WHICH GENRE WERE WE?

I wanted to write a spy thriller
you as the leading man
with virile strength
and chiselled intelligence
though you lacked the jaw.

But where could it have ended?
the little wedding chapel, leaving Las Vegas
a honeymoon with Elvis
slot machines
an exorcism in your church?

You said it was sweet
but really it was sweaty
slippery bodies that
moulded together
again and again
despite the dry desert heat
on the road
fear and loathing
out of Las Vegas

I was already ghosted
美国鬼
you the unrecognisable alien

They said the cold war was over
but that is how we ended
until the two towers fell
I reached out to see if you had to fight a real war.

It would have been a satisfying ending to my book
an HBO series with
you, the ill-fated hero.

美国鬼 mei gok gwei (Cantonese) – American devil

CLICHÉD RHIZOMES

in the humid vacuum of
lipped orchids and pink slings
sans histoire
nessun posto
appropriated modern myths
experimental voices

then JFK junior crashed his plane
when we drove through a land of
conspiracies; the valleys of death
lit by the nuclear neon sunset
flatland out of Vegas.

our soundtracks were never the same
and I, interpellated into narratives by
angsty white American men,
hid my love
of melodious ballads

I fumbled for an ending
on the drive back to the ranch
there was only talk of
sheds of onions
and how good mushrooms tasted when fried

the denouement was ordinary
small talk about cannibals
crossing Sierra Nevada Mountains
feigned expected revulsion.

The exposition was good, wasn't it?
But it was better when we were truly strangers.

BY THE WESTERN DOOR

brown sky day
submerged in sandy dust
fog of coal
        I pass out
no one knows
that I am here in bed
inhaling emissions of
面的 from the ring road below
in toxic dreams
        I kiss the golden green-eyed
boy who decodes in a command ship of
        the enemy state …
            fully clothed immodest …
                … we kiss again and again
in a grey concrete cubicle …
                … an ablution block
overlooking valleys of the giants
            … at the end of the
old world
new world   order

            before overt cyberwars

        he tastes warm
        fresh mint syncretic paste
            in acid-free tank-water rain.

only another's memory of a pendulous corpse
        shocks
            me into wakefulness that
        my love turns cold
            at cold war's end

goodbye Blue Ridge Mountains
Shenandoah River and the American dream.

面的 miàn di (Mandarin) – 'bread loaf taxi'[13]

BETWEEN THE STARS

Beyond the galaxy
Comic book
Blockbuster
Green screen blinds

Like Sandra Bullock lost in dark matter
        [preferable to the one lost in translation]
Finding a wormhole
                Go back in time

But which time beyond time?
 to the time of Lucy Australopithecus
        for diamond skies.
 or to Lucy.
祖母
christened by missionaries who unbound her feet.

No.
I want to go back to a time before 祖母 and early wo/man,
to the time when single-celled organisms multiplied.
I want to see the dawn of time.

祖母 zǔ mǔ (Mandarin) – paternal grandmother

RED, WHITE, BLUES

in my imagined homeland,
i live near the peak
but should i tan

               would
                    fall.

                            debased.

if i had stayed in that land
my imagined, the real land
i would not be here where
               forehead to forehead
               foreigners in a pit
               in ritual
               in a panopticon
               perimeter of PLA
               lost to EDM
               some on MDMA
               breathe industrial air

even Huxley could not dream of this
     [and you thought Amaurot was strange].

in my imagined homeland
i kneel in a row
alongside others robed in silk
practising sword play

               filtered through the lens of
               Christopher Doyle
               directed by fifth-generation directors

I want something more exotic.

BY THE EASTERN DOOR

stumble [into the haze]
find the classical music
      faux baroque café
      feminine rococo
      clean lines are overrated
shamelessly bat your eyes
              [one single lid the other double]

  at the punk rocker who serves brandy

there will be misunderstandings of course

      but there is brandy and cream
      and a native
      with a lilting Irish tongue
      我们马上关门儿
      然后又去那儿.

我们马上关门儿 wǒmen mǎ shān guānmén er (Mandarin) – we are closing soon
然后又去那儿 ránhòu yòu zài nà er (Mandarin) – where to after?

HEAVENLY PIECE

know nothing. hear nothing
monkey see, monkey do not
only speak of monkey in zoo
or monkey Wuhong 西游记
and of the man who speaks in tongues

        monkey do not hear
        monkey wants to stay
        monkey knows
        how monkey sing

        Allegro Vivace never
        Molto Grave minor key

but monkey knows no add B
      no add E
       no add D
        and A flat?

      no raised 7th [unless it's dominant]

for it would be too sad and
remind people that
people used to eat

        monkey brains raw.

西游记 sai yau gei (Cantonese) – Journey to the West[14]

唐

抵死　　　　　打死

听话

Monkey

No!

No nothing?

¯_(ツ)_/¯

唔　m (Cantonese) – a negative prefix
抵死　dai sei (Cantonese) – serves one right
打死　da sei (Cantonese) – beat to death
听话　teng wa (Cantonese) – obedient

IMPULSE BUYS

my face blended in with the others
yet I was silenced as my voice
was too foreign to barter

a dozen uni-ball pens
One custom-made 印章
(made with faux jade for tourists)
a dozen masks in pink sachets, the
ingredients – unknown to illiterate me

back in our dorm,
we mix the cherry blossom scented
powder with 温水 from my thermos
mix the paste with our fingers
in plastic bowls
not knowing if the mixture is
concocted in animal testing labs,
leftover flour, or worse.

we become negatives of blackface
when the mask solidifies
our faces are smoother and paler

we pick off the plaster to reveal
the same faces

we are still brownish olive or
olivey brown
for it's summer
and
I am still Chinese.

印章 yìn zhāng (Mandarin) – seal
温水 wan seui (Cantonese) – warm water

THE EMPRESS

They melted her during the war
but she returned after
to a typhoon shelter for fishermen
and my childhood park
She remained after 1997

One day she'll be niche
for hipsters
after 2047 I guess.
a tourist attraction
or study on consumption in the 19th century
when there was a union

or maybe they will throw her
into molten steel with the T-1000

I hope that when that time comes
there will still be trees
and children will play in the park again.

SMOOTH CRIMINALS REVISITED

it was seaweed
they fed on that; not
on despair and men
the sirens do not
bare their breasts for your viewing
pleasure nor strike deals with
ocean devils to plot your demise.

they do not sing for you.

tongue louse
replaced the little one's tongue.

no sirens nor mermaids were sacrificed
in the original
the sea witch was their elder
Disneyfication led to her demise.

Poseidon possesses no GPS
for they do what they will

it was not their fault you were lashed to the mast

It's convenient though isn't it.
that fecund temptresses
must have
            their wings clipped,
                        kow tow,
                                    below the line

...

            or die.

TAMPA TANKA

Obduracy is strength.
Mute the tears of babies' friends.
Encircle the land.
Isolate the air we breathe.
Neural pathways die in heat.

BOXING DAYS

Anonymous brown bodies in colourful death shrouds
Anonymous bodies laid out in a row
Anonymous bodies covered with cheap orange plastic
Officials examine bodies like I examine fish at the
Sydney fish market on Christmas Eve

Deep-water fish survive but those swept up
left stranded on the shore do not
battered to death
forces of nature

I know who the Swedish boy was
but not the others.
It's always the poor who die
The trailer park people swept away in floods
Roads washed away.

Neptune was indiscriminate
but those raptured still say
that God was punishing
us all for their sins.

Then there was Fukushima
And still some say, it was
because of
the Emperor

Others said that he was sorry
but it was too late
By then, curtains of bamboo and iron
formed a shield against new enemies.

Even sex tourists
are redeemed by such deaths
enclosed in body bags

If I were anywhere but here, would they try to identify me
or would my corpse be stockpiled?
celui-ci ou celui-là
farang or 本地人

本地人 běn dì rén (Mandarin) – local

GODS OF TE ANAU

It is too dangerous to drive
without snow chains
especially when they are
strung together with beaded plastic earrings
my sacrifice to the mountain gods
a gift from students
now old enough to be young grandmothers

my lover hesitates
unstrings the earrings
flags down a ute
'it's the back wheels,' the man says
I disagree but
there is now doubt.
There is always doubt.
Even when I'm away from my flat dry homeland.

It really doesn't make a difference
these are old tyres.

We drive up a fenceless god
and look down upon the mortals.

DAY ROAD

no one wants to see you
when did the rubies fade,
fall from your tears
clichéd fires.
the man who guides you out
of the static startles
sleepwalking secrets.

if you believed in the world
you wouldn't be here
unfurling your loins
your owner was once
the same
only nineteen
when she went was picked up
by a yellow-hound at a war memorial
a shared interest in history

identity is malleable
do you have the luxury of fate?

And whence such fair garments, such prosperity? –
O didn't you know I'd been ruined? said she[15]

NATIONAL TREASURES COMING HOME

My boss, the head nurse, says she has a collection of Ming dynasty crockery,
>Qing dynasty snuff bottles and
>a Shang 代 bronze tripod vase
>(always filled with fresh pomegranates)
>looted by her ancestors or
>bought at Sotheby's
>for all the tea in China.
>'I'm the poor cousin, the others got more
>Come for dinner and you'll see them all.'

I disliked her then, I dislike her now
>But it is Queen Victoria I should 更 讨厌
>throw rotten eggs at
>or spray *Four Bandits* on the pedestal where
>she sits in the park at the end of Great George Street.
>'Looty' was her Pekingese,
>say it in Cantonese '北京狗!'

It is my boss, not Victoria, who wants me to eat beef stroganoff and polenta
>off my ancestor's plates.
>sniff the potpourri she's placed
>in rhinoceros-shell-lined bottles
>translate the inked poems
>about ancient fish
>and explain why the toad has red eyes
>flared nose and only three legs

For dessert she will make a pavlova in her new Bosch oven
>with fresh cherries, seconds from local farms.

代 dài (Mandarin) – generation
更 讨厌 gèng tǎo yàn (Mandarin) – more disgusted
北京狗 bak ging gau (Cantonese) – Pekingese dog

I usually pay to admire stolen goods, encased in glass cabinets,
      national treasures and ancient clays I cannot afford to buy.
      I've seen the Egyptian treasures, excavated
      by the men who live in Downtown Abbey
      'Your Chinese mouth would not touch these Chinese treasures
      had we not salvaged history back to Portsmouth.
      Look at what happened to the Temple of Baalshamin
      the Giant Buddhas of Bamiyan!'

We have an understanding, she and I.
      I order pens, paper, ink cartridges and pantry supplies, soaps,
      malted milk and chocolate biscuits
      for children who attend our geriatric clinic.
      I add two extra boxes of tampons
      'For the patients, of course'
      I nod when she says, 'People *should* pay for their health care.'
      Because she gives me hour-long lunch breaks
      and calls me good girl
      I say, 'I will come to dinner.'

I will see if Russian gravy tastes better on centuries-old porcelain plates
      patterned by cobalt and manganese
      and ingest the same trace elements as
      imperial court nobles who ate 菜 off the
      crockery, fresh out of the kiln.

But my cousin says that our people were peasants who woke early to pick grains
      of rice or maybe it was wheat with our hands,
      we were foreign to the Forbidden City.
      I ask him what I should wear to a meal with the descendants
      of drug dealers who poisoned a nation with opioids
      rendered it sick
      too yellow and diseased
      to walk in leafy green meadows
      when they could not cure their addiction to yum cha.

菜 cài (Mandarin) – dishes of food

He says, 'I will lend you my vest, cut from the uniform of a Song dynasty eunuch.

It does not fit me but it will indeed fit you.'

Perhaps

Perhaps

Perhaps.

PSITHURISM

the statue spoke to you
the last time you were here
the trees around it whispered
'we are not evergreens
autumn leaves are
falling and soon we will be bald,
stripped bare, unwanted.
our beauty reduced to skeletal
proportions.
not everyone understands'.

I told them that the snow will fringe
their frail branches
and winter is temporary

'but you hate the cold' they swished
'go back to your evergreens
to the virgin karri
who remember the megafauna
to your white eucalyptus trees
there's no hope for you here.
stay away from weeping willows
the toad in toad hall hibernates'.

Go home
回家
回国
au revoir

But to where?

————————————

回家 huí jiā (Mandarin) – return home
回国 huí guó (Mandarin) – return to country

... CONTINUING ...

FRESHWATER SWAMPS

For Lake Street, Northbridge

Once an Emperor's Court
there were lower-rung concubines
runner maids
answerable to lipsticked mistresses
in 黑 旗袍,
sprinkled with cherry blossoms
slit to their lower thighs

I used to serve king crabs
cooked
(mostly) post-execution,
a welcome end to their plastic
tie lives.

at least the emperor did not
command that we
sell thrills of watching
lobsters as their tails twitch
eaten in sashimi style.

I almost rose through the ranks
To wear an *In the Mood for Love* dress
except I did not know how to
present the delicacies
and I could only wear boots.

Now it's a republic
for aspirational Mrs Batiatuses
titillated by cuffed men.

黑 旗袍 hak kei po (Cantonese) – black traditional Chinese dress

DISCLAIMER

I am not always
in the deepest pit of
angst
wallowing in a sea of
never ending laundry

                    I like to ponder how the
                    world spins and counts
                    seconds in the Paleocene
                    or ponder if other fauna know
                    before we do
                    of the next Great Dying.

These are simple needs
a break from the monotony of
car park rage
pseudo faces
happy children playing
burning hearths
bleached white

WE NEED TO TALK ABOUT IMMIGRATION ...

'It's unfair
this alternative path for 6000 others
but 6000 means
6000 more consumers
who will arrive
in the form of skilled migration
from England,
Ireland,
Scotland and Wales
and others who speak our language
of course.

But there may be fewer now from
the motherland, now happily
bereft of her continental children.
They couldn't understand her anyway,'
the logic-man says.

5757 is not 6000
And what of the other 7900
lives in limbo?

'There is no culture because
culture belongs to everyone.
We do not discriminate,'
a bestseller and an actress repeat.

I suppose what this means is that
I can live here as an accountant,

wear your trousers,
and that we can both sell 枸杞
as something more than
a pleasant weed
wah! 而家鬼佬识饮枸杞汤啊!

It's good for your kidneys,
nephrologists know
not phrenologists
that's the skull.

It means you can take my dialect,
shorten it and turn an affectionate
curse into playground chants
about dirty Chinese laundry men

枸杞 gau gei (Cantonese) – goji plant
而家鬼佬识 饮枸杞汤啊! yi ga gwei lo sik yam gau gei tong ah! (Cantonese) –
    even white people know how to drink goji broth!

Everyone else looks the same to
them too: mediocre.

啊傻 啊傻
　　　　that makes the ABC cry but
　　　　the 大人就笑哈哈.

It's a love hate thing
And less clear cut with darker ghosts
as someone has to cushion
de Gobineau's base,
Verwoerd knew it.

privilege the light
even though it's the sun that burns

啊傻 ah sor (Cantonese) – a fool
大人就笑哈哈 dai yan zou ha ha siew (Cantonese) – the grown-ups laugh

SIAMESE CAT
For 妙儿

a bamboo ceiling.
    sits beneath the glass one
        change your facade for monolingual tongues
    green bamboo
        grows into
        clicketty clack, clicketty clack, clicketty clack
    flooring.

your face says country stays with everyone
        on this terrain.

    if you were in the east, would you surface or follow him?

猫功 mao gong 贸工.
you look to highlight these
    fresh wet markets, your translucent skin,
        the remote lush valleys.
Juxtapositions

    it's beautiful for the most part.
        it's pretty, weird, remote
          and extremely you.

    diverse within provinces of pine
landscapes of mountainous mountains

    but would you lead him wherever you go and
        mark stiletto dents on the soft hard floor?

    you say that I'm not a patriot
        and *that* is always a moral dilemma.

clicketty clack, clicketty clack, clicketty clack
above me.

猫功 maau gung (Cantonese) – 'cat' kongfu [a style of martial arts]
贸工 mào gong (Mandarin) – trade worker

DOPPELGÄNGER ACROSS LANDS
For G

Do you think we look like strangers?

When you sit on the couch, fold your right
arm across your left
so do I.

In your face I see my smile
in your laugh I hear my sardonic voice
the one that surfaces when we see something
on television
like Dutton announcing a new policy
of exclusion
Yet how can we look alike when you are
more Neanderthal than I?
we are apart yet we are together.

People say we look the same
but you are from the Iberian peninsular
and I am HAPLO M
somewhere in West Asia
I share a common ancestor
with those who have the Mongolian spot
and have distant relatives who do not eat pork
They have forgotten that we were
once from the same family
many great, great, and many more great-grandmothers ago.

Maybe our ancestors sat together in caves
then during the Bronze Age
scattered to find greener pastures
or perhaps when Marco Polo's entourage
crossed into my ancestor's land
their DNA remained.

We have never been strangers.

NEW NEW SPEAK

I want you to know that we are trusting the beginning
In a way that much a decision
The implementation of conditions are thus.

You must agree which the obligations will disrupt
The status quo upon which time
The moratorium still stands.

Clients do not condone allegations
Lest we are undone by lengthy insurance claims
Against deadline disease, death and destiny.

PALATABLE

You sitting on country,
feed on truffle oil upon
lightly sautéed rare Wagyu
slices balanced upon potatoes
smashed upon black radish fiddle
head and plated
grapes sourced from the Great Southern
aromatic spicy
little foie gras
fig and mint

you commit to paper, a story
melanges of history
whisked and baked into a digitally
timed meringue.

Let me take you back a century
to tell a story that is neither of ours
but more mine than yours.
It's easier with hindsight
confirmed causality.

all events have come to pass
but you still do not grasp the horror
when telling a story with roots in starvation
nor know any of the
the famished who ate leather belts and
seeds from droppings.

you focus instead on
an Indigenous prostitute
and a funny little Chinaman.

easy tropes.

VIRTUS

I wish I could remember what
faith wore to the dance,
or hope,
why chastity was there
for charity?

they were in all in the hall
sipping Shirley Temples
freshly laundered
cotillion gloves.

BONUS BABY

my friend is content
a second baby girl
she will have a third
and Peter 叔叔 says he will
cover some costs:
a Baby Björn, Bugaboo
and maid service in Bali.

she wants a boy for her husband
There something ingrained within
that makes her want to create a penis
to recompense her parents' disappointment
when they first knew she was just a girl.

Costello wants him for the nation.

叔叔 sook sook (Cantonese) – uncle

打完 仗总会有和平

For Rika

We are supposed to be enemies
according to modern history and
21st century politicians
yet she is more supportive
than my *own people*
came back from Beijing to register.

religious fundamentalists
urge their congregation to bleed for me
not for the kingdom of heaven
for there is no redemption through good deeds
alongside producers looking for a good story
somewhere in the chase for ratings
could there be a beating heart?

must I belong? can I belong with
so many incongruencies?
and this is why I hold onto
songs without words
the only logic that appeals

打完 仗总会有和平 da yun jeung jung wui yau wo ping (Cantonese) –
after war there is peace

her father, born to '死日本仔' in China
shares a cup of genmaicha with
my war father:
a witness to 死日本仔 pouring
honey into the eyes of the villagers
bound to stakes in the tropical sun
delicacies for jungle ants
they speak not of dehydration.

creationists and atheists share a joke in
my hospital room — not about dinosaurs
a settler and activist wish me well
weep at my misfortune
but there is still the wall
and I am on neither side.

as my cells wage war within my future corpse
We are truly in the post post world.

_____

死日本仔 sei yat bun zai (Cantonese) – 'dead Japanese' [pejorative]

NORWEGIAN WOULD

It couldn't happen here.
They're insane
Or abused
Or abused and insane
Or abusing
Distorted brain chemistry
Nothing to worry about
No one likes Mondays
Relax mate, people only go to Forrest Chase for Boxing Day sales.
Apathy is not our saviour
It must be the weather
Why would you shoot the whole day down when you can laze on
the beach?

DOUBLE EXOTIC 囍

In Old Shanghai
they sit around a hot pot in Old Shanghai
an invitation to dress Asian
- paper furoshiki
- bamboo chopsticks
- a novel about dreams and tea house
- a calligraphy set
- me?

he said he wanted to fish
with cormorants and old Guilin men

had he been any paler and his
ancestors held any
larger concessions
nor had the looks to
step out of an Armani ad or
complement the
cobbled streets of Milan
throw three coins in a fountain
with Audrey
I would not have held out hope
for breakfast nor said
che coincidenza;
quando sorridi, gli angeli
piangono, è così bello

and had he understood,
he would not have replied
你的电话号码是多少?

we now grow dragon fruits together
                    below the Tropic of Capricorn.

囍 xǐ (Mandarin) – double happiness
你的电话号码是多少? nǐ dǐe diàn huà hào shì duō shǎo? (Mandarin) –
   what's your phone number?

PROPERTY RIGHTS

How can it be that history begins here
     If we could reclaim what is ours
      Could I reclaim a house, a street
an entire village, a province?

No.
Because I lack a phallus
the signifier that I should be owner of lands
and my mother lacks one
as did hers.

If I could go back
before the revolutions I would
be a peasant with the freedom of unbound feet
or a girl
training to trot on tiptoes
bound feet
trained to arouse
titillate my husband's g-spot.

I am happy to stay in this time
Lie on this dried grass
patched over dunes
breathe clean air
(with your permission of course)
until the ocean reclaims the shore.

UNDER THE DOME

A café of people
who voted for Brexit
but will never return to the Isle

I search faces for some recognition
hilarity
familiarity
similarity
beyond our thin layers of sweatshop cloth
and past admin jobs where
we all licked 英女王 stamps
back when there was a 太茶夫人.

> If we were together on exile beach or in a classroom
> would you reach out to me?
> I heard your voice once
> 'maaate' and you made me feel safe,
> I fell for it
> before I realised it was conditional
> and that I had to say it back to you
> in the way that you wanted me to say it
>
> would you help me start the fire?
> or would I have to join
> the running dogs of Empires?
>
> To seal the deal,
> I will show you my caesarean scar
> And you will find that I am exactly
> the right type of exotic.

英女王 ying neui wong (Cantonese) – British Queen (Queen Elizabeth II)
太茶夫人 taai cha fu yan (Cantonese) – 'Tea Madam' (Margaret Thatcher)

VERISIMILITUDE

one story …
        no. not that one
I know which one you want
… not the soy bean in tetra pak one
  nor the one made with industrial steel.
         you want authenticity
         and me to cook and grind and squeeze
             the milk through cheesecloth
             not me
        the white-sage
                she cleaned your office

             now a commodity
             like coconut water
             or companionship
             bone broth

COME VISIT US?

I will pick you up from the station because
you wear a head scarf for reasons other than
complete hair loss through chemotherapy.

if you choose to walk to my place
you need to have that *je ne sais quoi* stride
                    especially when you walk past the
                            house with the 'Love it or Leave it' SUV.

I will pick you up from the station
It's not because of the old man who
haunts the footpaths with a pitchfork.
                    He is the friendly neighbourhood watch.

I will pick you up from the station
Then a tequila sunrise sunset where
            I'll show you the secret coves only locals know.

I must pick you up from the station because
I've been cursed with the smile and people
share with me their ugly thoughts that I wish
would remain encased in their skulls.

            I can walk home from the station because they've seen
                    my gaffer-taped home

            After I pick you up from the station
                    we can eat fish and chips,
                    squeal with glee when
                            the seals
                    arise from their slumber and
                        bake in the sun,
                    the good doctor cools the land
                    the Indian ocean white caps
                    gently lambadas to the shore

Text me when you leave.

TOUR GUIDE

glass towers of industry
supranational pride
I emerge from hibernation
on a hot winter's day.

> here is our museum which opens next decade.
> we now have four bubble tea franchises
> along William Street. a state theatre.
> authentic dumplings. and of course, the
> yellow vests on bikes are here for your safety.
> but I don't know what is happening
> over there and why they surround a group of
> tween boys or why there are four of them. I
> used to teach 32 children at one time. If you
> say this is excessive even by LA standards,
> let's walk a bit closer and make sure they are
> ok

Excuse me officer, I can't help but notice that these children have
no guardian.
Excuse me officer, but can you approach children and speak to
them in this way without an adult present?
Excuse me officer, why is that very large colleague of yours asking
the young boy to spread like a starfish in the middle of the mall?
Excuse me officer, is he allowed to remove the boy's jacket?
Excuse me officer, it's the business owners who called you *but did
you know I'm a customer and I was busy shopping alongside
these boys?*
Excuse me officer, are you saying that you can move on anyone,
any age, any time?
Excuse me officer, why do businesses think these children scare
tourists?
Excuse me officer, is your colleague allowed to touch that boy in
that way?
I know it's a pat down so did you think he took something?

Excuse me officer, I can't help but notice that all these boys have
tanned skin …
What? You arrest me?
Oh no sir, I don't mean to obstruct you, a police officer.
I'm so sorry officer, I'm not from around here. I do not know your
laws and my English is not so good but I know accents. Yours is
from Northern England? Manchester? Midlands? Who me? I'm
nobody tourist.

I walk away.
Pale yellow skin guilt.

STARRY NIGHT, WARD 9

she once walked in beauty, like the night,
and near death her heart of love is innocent
we are all purified by fast replicating cells.

we repent
we repent

she does not go gently into the night
instead coughs and coughs up
tubercle bacilli through
the filtered air
filthy from the full commode

we repent
we repent

under the microscope consumption looks
like handmade fideos
paella without rice

we repent
we repent

elevated above it all
I sit cross-legged, open palms on knees
not quite bhumisparsha mudra
there is no bodhi tree
so there can be no enlightenment
on a hydraulic bed.

we repent
we repent

anger subsides
as euphoria rises
breathing deeply through
nasal tubes awaiting
promised salvation
in the form of carcinogens
fanta-like,
a liquid to kill them all

we repent
we repent

ONCE UPON A TIME ...

C-H-I-N-A-M-A-N
was Rohmer's ouija board
that made him create
Fu Manchu, a man who couldn't even
do it.
Sent in his [female] assistants.
It was a long time ago, a different era.

reality TV joke
William Hung
singing idiot, infantile clown
but Simon Cowell is kinder now, it was a different era.

or that Toni Collette film
about iron ore
her Japanese lover
dives into and drowns

other people drown in billabongs
it doesn't only take the lives of oriental men

but the swagman's fall into cavernous waters
was consensual
under the shade of the coolabah tree

his ghost can still be heard, enigmatic
but Hiromitsu never rose
from the dead
It's the Chinese who demand ore now. That was a long time ago.

Remember when Tarantino
killed Bill? He sent in a Nordic blonde
in Little Dragon's yellow suit and before you
say that that was also a long time ago,
he castrated the dragon this summer.
And that is the curse of the dragon.

THEY ARE NOW OUR CUSTOMERS

In Middlesex
I sink into dark blue plastic
chairs amongst pre-pubescent
Londoners, travellers, Sinti, Afghani
Christian Congolese,
disputed despoted territories

Far from the
cacophony of chaos
planes destined for
the sky roar above us

Orphaned
cherubic faces find
safety in
rhyme. Rhythm
away from tanks
tankas, haikus, cinquains.
The moonlight shines upon
her deceased mother's bindi
Osama Bin Laden
Is he good or bad miss?
Kamikaze is never a good thing.

Back home
I explain to Wendi
that there are many exceptions
to the rules
then the teenage man with acetous breath
edits
Versace, Ferrari and real estate
in his/our [?] mother tongue asks
why 老师 why
the present, the past and the perfect?

老师 lǎo shī (Mandarin) – teacher

and what I think of a candle
encircled by barb wires
and umbrellas
black t-shirts
yellow vests and one-eyed bandits

>   *Do I dare disturb the universe, then burn the*
>   *suspension bridge?*

I check my deposit, the real estate,
my EBA and the fees they pay
to go beyond their A, B, Cs

English is a bastardised language anyways.

妈妈为什么?

'The atom bomb killed victims three times'
  – Yishoro Yamawaki, Nagasaki Survivor[16]

Sadako died before she folded
her one thousand paper cranes
with scraps

妈妈为什么?
because of Oppenheimer
because of the bomb
because of Enola Gay
because of Truman
because of the Emperor
because of man
                  we live in peace now

                  妈妈为什么?
                  because the towers fell
                  because of terrorists
                  because of wars that started
                  because of other wars
                  because of man's true nature
                  it also happens to babies
                  rocked to sleep
                  in their mother's arms
                  because of a mutation
                  because of the glitch in the matrix
                  because cells replicate and colonise

                  妈妈为什么你还在这里?
                  because of the trials
                  because of rodents

妈妈为什么? mämä wèi shé me (Mandarin) – why mummy?
妈妈为什么你还在这里? mä mä wèi shé me nǐ hái zài zhè li (Mandarin) –
  why mummy are you still here?

because of chemistry
because of vesicant gas
because some survived the attack
and took weeks to die

I am alive because of war.

NEWBORN AUSTRALIAN

East must be East, West must be West
now twain entwines the 混血
don't call him 杂种, don't call him *mulatto* or
claim him as theirs because of his higher brows and nose
who else can he be but yours … ours?

the judgement of home affairs may differ
from that of King Solomon.

混血 hùn xiě (Mandarin) – mixed race
杂种 jaap jung (Cantonese) – mixed-breed [pejorative]

ON MY WAY TO TEMPURA UDON

His statue
looks afar
past the freeway entrance
over my old high school
to cooler country
past swamps on the way to the Indian Ocean.

alas on this mid-spring day
he is concretised
at a meeting place for little
girls who dream of wearing
polyester aquamarine and pink
ball gowns and beastly princes.
melting ice-creams during the
holidays.

people seek refuge in
(mostly) rectangular prisms reaching for a sky
reflected in blue mirrored towers some
brutalist
shelter.

the peppermint trees
too young to offer relief
where have all the flowers gone?
now only the doctor can cool
this fan-forced oven.

what would Midgegooroo have thought?

SO WHAT IF I SMASH A BOWL?

the nurse said to keep all the connections alive … now they say you
overthink … but what is the baseline … I love you … I love you …
death anxiety is normal … death is normal … is thinking about
death normal … normal for us … normal for some… irrational
here but in the natural world there are predators … lions. tigers.
bears … not ebay scammers … ticket scalpers … it's too much …
it's too much … one little person cannot solve war … famine …
melting icebergs … gyres in the ocean … or the sun exploding in
billions of years' time … facts … so why is this neural atypical …
industrial copying from 9 to 3 … what happened to the trees … it
was easier … when i could keep you safe … and you were my little
analgesic and i yours … and you believed in magical dragons and
santa claus … now he's an intruder at night … reading is no longer
reading … it is data … reading is money … money is god now.
it is too much.
it is too much.
it is too much.
it is now survival of the anesthetised.

INITIALISMS

ADD OCD ADHD
Inattentive
ASD
GATE
IEP
AEP
ERB
TRB

for funding
for convenience
for meaning

comfort in correlations
from conception to caesarean
to explain data
consumer knowledge
consumer knows
consumer
consumes
NAP LAN
ICAS
PISA
TIMMS [Tam]
WISC
Whiskey
TGIF

Too much
KFC
IHOP
IKEA needs no reinvention
buy buy buy
We cheap[er]
No patient patients
From PAC to CAC
patient care
consumer knowledge
consumer knows
consumer
consumes
consumption

IMA
I'M A
I MA?
… what of humanity?

a game of balderdash

SSRIs
ECT
a stopgap
panacea.

TEMPORALITY

I cannot be a Buddhist
nor accept the noble truths for
I do not believe that the runner-up prize
to living noble life is to become human
again
and again
and I know that pleasure is fleeting
that only aging, illness and death
are certain and that the deadly sins
are born out of ignorance
and lack of awareness
and I accept that all life ends

I pray
but there were too many gods
and versions of God offered to me
and not all came with John's head
on a platter

and I pray in all temples
listen to the pentatonic chants
and have studied the Roman and Greeks
and Viking gods
and in ancient churches and
I know why
why we need the explanation
the story and the saviour

I can pray for your soul
in multiple realms
be soothed by your well-wishing tongues
but if Charles II didn't make up his mind
until his dying breath

                    why should I?

WANDERING MINSTREL IN TRANSLATION[17]

he travels from south to north
from black to white
did you know? did you really know?
everyone sees him
but does not know who he is

he returns home when the alarm sounds
a sigh of regret
tries to find meaning in his dark skin
I want everyone to see me
but not know who I am
when we say goodbye
for the last time in the rain

colour struggle, life's sacrifice
loss of possession
yet there is still hope
if you see me a little tired
pour me some water
ancient drums for one nation
if you have already fallen in love with me
just kiss me on my lips
in ancient times there was a dragon
a yellow river of sorrow

little Lee was the romantic swordsman
from another house of
flying daggers, a hero
Roman was the godfather of pop.

a Chinese Delores
lingers in dreams
let's hug for a minute
And kiss for ten.

mashup of notes
my sentiment's
the same.

WHAT DID THE FOX SAY?

I went to Chinatown
not in Haymarket
and not in Soho
nor the 13th arrondissement

this time it
was everything I ever wanted
transported back to ancient times
mini Song dynasty
stalls of real and plastic dumplings
noodles and buns for an old beggar
dynastic guards
and a mega star
blue green screen for more
imaginings from the mind of
American dollars and
sense to include those who need
no kohl to accentuate their
almond eyes
they call them almond now.

Suspended in studio time
alongside dentists, lawyers and architects who
marvel at our fabricated world
I want to stay here forever.

No one
in this world
had bound feet

and there he was
again outside my trailer
in his Song dynasty garb.

123 ... 321 ... 1234567
        234 ... 432 ... 456789 10

                4 ... 3 ... 0 ... go rocket ...

                    Let's go!

TRIBAL AFFILIATIONS

… … then she said:

… my mother's mother's father was … …

           … and from a non–pork eating minority …

… it's why your great uncle was mistaken for a gweilo

           … he taught English at a university … …

he cried when the government took away his books …

               Where?

… Which group? …

… Who? …   … What university? …

… Whose government?   Which country?

When? … … …   … Which era? … … …

… … there is no reply … … … …

NOTES

詠 (yǒng) means to hum, to chant, or to sing, and is the verb used to describe the recitation of ancient Chinese poetry. It is also my name.

Although I have used simplified Chinese throughout this collection, my name remains in traditional Chinese. I have used the pin yin for transliteration of Mandarin and my own system for other dialects. All grammatical disruptions in this collection are intentional.

1. 'Causeway Bay': 大丸 is Daimaru, the Japanese department store which opened in Hong Kong on Great George Street in 1960 and closed down in 1998.

2. 'Maybe it's Wanchai': There are two popular Hong Kong actors named Tony Leung. Tony Leung Ka-Fai is known to Western audiences for his role in the 1992 film adaptation of Marguerite Duras' French colonial novel *The Lover*, and Tony Leung Chiu-Wai for his role in Ang Lee's 2007 film adaptation of Eileen Chang's 1979 novella 色, 戒 (*Lust, Caution*).

3. 'Maybe it's Wanchai': 香蕉船 (The Banana Boat) was a Hong Kong children's television show produced by public broadcasting station RTHK between 1979 and 1984. 香蕉 (banana) is used to describe diasporic Chinese who are 'yellow on the outside but white on the inside'. The term is can be interpreted as both pejorative and a compliment.

4. 'Romeo would, were he not Romeo Call'd': Wei refers to Lady Wei Shou (272–349) who introduced the theory of calligraphy by breaking it down into seven key brushstrokes. Her principles were later developed into the 'Eight Principles of Yong'. To this day, calligraphers promote the practice of writing 永 (yǒng) as the character includes the eight basic strokes of Chinese calligraphy.

5. 'Ah! vous dirai-je, Maman!': 'Ah! should I tell you, Mummy!'
   The title of a popular French folk song set to the tune of
   'Twinkle Twinkle Little Star'.

6. 'Long Grove': Long Grove Hospital (1907–1992) was an English
   mental health institution in Epsom, Surrey, also known as
   Long Grove Asylum and Long Grove Mental Hospital.

7. 'Bedtime Stories': 'Momotaro's Song' is a Japanese folk song
   about a giant-slaying little boy, born from a peach. My father
   learned it during the Japanese occupation of Malaya during
   the Second World War, and he often sang it to me when I was a
   young child.

8. '怪怪了': I first heard the fragment '怪怪了' in a song introduced
   to me by someone in the underground music scene in late
   twentieth century Beijing.

9. 'Impromptu': 阿里山的姑娘' ('The Maiden from Alishan
   Mountains') is the commonly used name for the song '高山
   青' ('High Green Mountains'). The song, composed by film
   director 张撤 (Zhang Che) for his 1949 movie 阿里山的风
   云 (Storm Clouds at Alishan Mountains), gained popularity
   within diasporic Chinese communities after Taiwanese pop
   star Teresa Teng covered the song in the 1970s. Found in most
   Chinese language karaoke bar catalogues, the song has been
   criticised for misappropriating traditional Tsao – the group
   indigenous to Alishan – language and culture.

10. 'Vociferate': 三从四德 (three obediences, four virtues) refers to
    the Confucian code that required women to obey their father
    before marriage, husband after marriage, and the first son after
    she was widowed. Women, according to this code, should also
    possess the four virtues: 妇德 (female virtues), 妇言 (feminine
    speech), 妇容 (feminine appearances) and 妇功 (female work).
    In short, the ideal woman was one who knew that she was
    inferior to men, of average appearance and intelligence, did
    not talk too much, and was a good wife and mother.

11. The title 'Six Two Six' refers to Wolfgang Amadeus Mozart's *Requiem Mass K 626*. Mozart composed this work on his deathbed in 1791.

12. 东南西北中发白 are mahjong tiles which some call 'honour suits'. The 'wind' suit comprises 东南西北 east, south, west, north tiles and 中发白 make up what English speakers call the 'dragon' suit. These tiles use traditional Chinese characters and so will appear as: 東南西北中發 on modern mahjong tiles. 白 is usually a white rectangle with a blue outline.

13. 'By the Western Door': 面的 or 'bread taxis' were affordable yellow mini-van taxis in 1980s and 1990s Beijing.

14. 'Heavenly Piece': *Journey to the West*, the novel attributed to Ming dynasty novelist Wu Cheng'en, is one of the four classics of Chinese literature.

15. 'Day Road': '"And whence such fair garments, such prosperity?" – "Oh didn't you know I'd been ruined?" said she' is from Thomas Hardy's 1866 poem 'The Ruined Maid'.

16. '妈妈为什么?': Yishoro Yamawaki is one of the people featured in *TIME Magazine*'s photo essay 'After the Bomb: Survivors of the Atomic Blasts in Hiroshima and Nagasaki Share their Stories', time.com/after-the-bomb.

17. 'Wandering Minstrel in Translation': This poem is a mashup of my own translations of misheard Chinese song lyrics. Some fragments may be more accurate than others.

ACKNOWLEDGEMENTS

Excerpt from *Orientalism* by Edward W. Said, copyright ©1978 by Edward W. Said is used by permission of Pantheon Books, an imprint of the Knopf Doubleday Publishing Group, a division of Penguin Random House LLC. All rights reserved.Cover image, 丽 珠 by C.Y. Sun, copyright ©1968, is used with permission of the photographer.

I want to thank the editors of *Australian Poetry Journal*, *Cordite Poetry Review*, *Hecate*, *Mascara Literary Review*, *The Sky Falls Down: An Anthology of Grief*, *Meanjin*, *Meniscus* and *Westerly*, where earlier versions of some poems in this collection have appeared.

My sincere and heartfelt thanks to Tracy Ryan and Georgia Richter for their guidance, to Anna Maley-Fadgyas for her design, and to Fremantle Press for taking a risk with this collection.

Thank you also to Nadia Rhook, Marianna Shek, Carol Millner and Mikaela Nyman for their support throughout this project, Alice Pung and Rashida Murphy for imbuing me with the confidence to publish this work, Laurie Steed for encouraging me to write about my hometown Perth, and Qian Gong for introducing me to the joys of translanguaging in poetry. Thank you too to Anne Surma for inspiring my intellectual curiosity.

I would also like to acknowledge the significant role that the Centre for Stories' Inclusion Matters program, the Katharine Susannah Prichard Writers' Centre, and the Deborah Cass Prize for Writing play in welcoming voices such as mine into the Australian literary landscape.

Finally, I could not have written this book without the love and support of my family, especially my parents who shared with me their rich histories and allowed me the freedom to interpret them in whichever way I chose. For this, I am eternally grateful.

First published 2021 by
FREMANTLE PRESS

Fremantle Press Inc. trading as Fremantle Press
25 Quarry Street, Fremantle WA 6160
(PO Box 158, North Fremantle WA 6159)
www.fremantlepress.com.au

Cover photograph 丽珠 by C.Y. Sun.
Printed by Lightning Source.

A catalogue record for this
book is available from the
National Library of Australia

ISBN 9781760990220 (paperback)
ISBN 9781760990237 (ebook)

Fremantle Press is supported by the State Government through the
Department of Local Government, Sport and Cultural Industries.

Publication of this title was assisted by the Commonwealth Government
through the Australia Council, its arts funding and advisory body.

Printed in Australia
AUHW021237010921
351361AU00003B/3

9 781760 990220